YOUR
CHANGING BRAIN
A Guidebook

BY JEFF SZPIRGLAS AND
DANIELLE SAINT-ONGE

CRABTREE
PUBLISHING COMPANY
WWW.CRABTREEBOOKS.COM

CRABTREE
PUBLISHING COMPANY
WWW.CRABTREEBOOKS.COM

Authors: Jeff Szpirglas, Danielle Saint-Onge

Series Research and Development: Reagan Miller

Editors: Janine Deschenes, Kenneth Lane

Proofreader: Wendy Scavuzzo

Design: Margaret Amy Salter

Photo research: Margaret Amy Salter

Production coordinator and
 Prepress technician: Margaret Amy Salter, Abigail Smith

Print coordinator: Katherine Berti

Consultant: Kenneth Lane, Bioscientist and Science Writer and Editor

Acknowledgement: Eleanor A. Maguire FMedSci, FRS,
 University College London

Photo Credits
bl=bottom left

Shutterstock: ©StockStudio p 12

Wikimedia: p 7 (bl)

All other images from Shutterstock

Library and Archives Canada Cataloguing in Publication

Szpirglas, Jeff, author
    Your changing brain : a guidebook / Jeff Szpirglas,
Danielle Saint-Onge.

(Exploring the brain)
Includes bibliographical references and index.
Issued in print and electronic formats.
ISBN 978-0-7787-3499-4 (hardcover).--
ISBN 978-0-7787-3511-3 (softcover).--
ISBN 978-1-4271-1995-7 (HTML)

    1. Brain--Growth--Juvenile literature. 2. Brain--Physiology--
Juvenile literature. 3. Adolescent psychology--Juvenile literature. I.
Saint-Onge, Danielle, author II. Title.

QP376.S98 2017   j612.8'2   C2017-906549-1
                                                  C2017-906550-5

Library of Congress Cataloging-in-Publication Data

Names: Szpirglas, Jeff, author. | Saint-Onge, Danielle, 1982- author.
Title: Your changing brain : a guidebook / Jeff Szpirglas and
    Danielle Saint-Onge.
Description: New York, New York : Crabtree Publishing Company,
    [2018] | Series: Exploring the brain | Includes bibliographical
    references and index.
Identifiers: LCCN 2017059672 (print) | LCCN 2017060343 (ebook) |
    ISBN 9781427119957 (Electronic HTML) |
    ISBN 9780778734994 (reinforced library binding) |
    ISBN 9780778735113 (pbk.)
Subjects: LCSH: Brain--Growth--Juvenile literature. |
    Brain--Physiology--Juvenile literature. | Neurophysiology--
    Juvenile literature.
Classification: LCC QP376 (ebook) | LCC QP376 .S97 2018 (print) |
    DDC 612.8/2--dc23
LC record available at https://lccn.loc.gov/2017059672

Crabtree Publishing Company
www.crabtreebooks.com   1-800-387-7650

Printed in the U.S.A./022018/CG20171220

Published in Canada
Crabtree Publishing
616 Welland Ave.
St. Catharines, Ontario
L2M 5V6

Published in the United States
Crabtree Publishing
PMB 59051
350 Fifth Avenue, 59th Floor
New York, New York 10118

Published in the United Kingdom
Crabtree Publishing
Maritime House
Basin Road North, Hove
BN41 1WR

Published in Australia
Crabtree Publishing
3 Charles Street
Coburg North
VIC, 3058

Table of Contents

CHAPTER 1

Your DEVELOPING Brain

This is your brain, the control hub for your entire body.

It's in charge of how you move, breathe, use your senses, and even how you think and process, or understand, information. For many years, scientists believed that the brain went through most of its development when you were very young—especially during the first five years of your life.

But advances in technology are now allowing us to look at the brain, and its changes, in much more detail. What we're now learning is that the brain continues to undergo and experience important changes throughout your life, and specifically during your adolescent (teenage) years. It's not just your body that is maturing and changing during adolescence, but also the way that you think, make decisions, and act upon them.

You have the power to play an active role in your brain development!

In this book, we'll crack through that skull of yours and get an in-depth look at the inner workings of your changing brain. What's physically happening to the various structures within your brain as you grow and age? And what impact do the environment and people around you have on your changing brain? What do you need to do to ensure that as you make healthy choices for growth, you're growing a healthy brain, too?

Research Advances

Some of the reasons we now know so much about the brain are because of the advances in science that have happened over the past several years. In this book, you'll read about studies in which **brain imaging technologies** are being to learn about how the brain can grow and change. But what are these technologies, and how are they used?

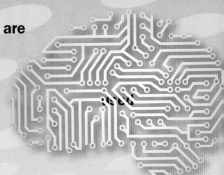

fMRI

Scientists can measure brain activity using a technique called **functional magnetic resonance imaging** (fMRI). fMRI uses a machine that maps brain activity by looking at how **oxygen** levels change in the blood that goes through the brain. That's because when brain areas are activated, they tend to use more oxygen. For example, you can increase the blood flow to the **motor region** of the brain by around 60% by quickly tapping each finger of one hand against your thumb. fMRI imaging is done in a special magnetic resonance imaging chamber.

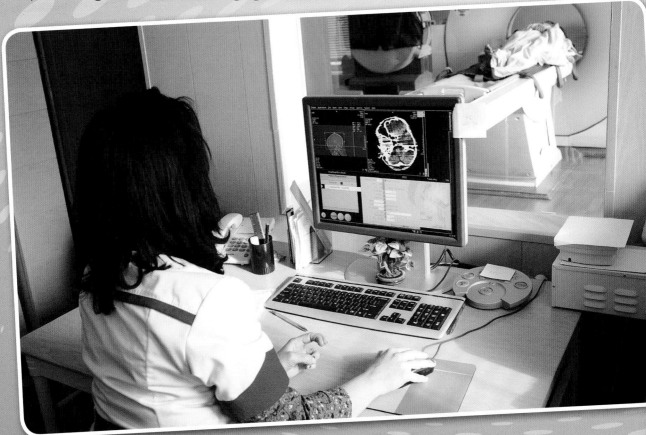

EEG

Electroencephalography (EEG) involves putting a series of **electrodes** on the scalp. From these, electrical signals can be picked up from the brain. The EEG amplifies these signals, or makes them bigger, and gives a reading of the electrical energy the brain produces. While fMRI shows a map of the brain, EEG readings are a series of jagged lines that show changes in brain activity over time. EEG tests can be used to help people suffering from seizures, head injuries, and even sleeping problems.

/85
3   SLC 6

92 MM

MG
GLU

10.4
9.8
9.2
8.6
8.1
7.5
6.9
6.3
5.7
5.1
4.5
4.0
3.4
2.8
2.2
1.6
1.0
0.5

PET

No, not "pet" like a dog or cat—but **positron emission tomography**. Although the PET scanner resembles the MRI and fMRI scanners, there's a difference. PET scans show how the tissues of the brain work by using a tracer, a kind of **radioactive** substance that is given by a **syringe**, and will travel through the blood. PET scans can help show brain cancers.

The Developing Brain

When you're born, you immediately need to begin making sense of the world around you through your senses, communicating through cries alone. Your brain undergoes significant changes during your first years of life. Here's a quick lowdown of what's going on in a young child's brain.

cell body

Neurons are connected to each other through **axons** and **dendrites**.

dendrites

axon

0–1 years old

The brain is made up of many **cells**. You're born with around 200 billion brain cells. Some brain cells are called **neurons**. These are connected to each other. Neurons carry messages within the brain and from the brain to other parts of the body. Each day, the brain of a baby grows by around 0.05 ounces (1.5 grams).

1–2 years old

By two years of age, the brain weighs around 80% of its adult weight.

2 years old and up

During the toddler years, the brain has around 100-trillion connections between different neurons.

4 years old

Your brain's energy consumption is huge—50% greater than when you're an adult. In proportion to your body weight, your brain also takes up much more space. By around 4 years old, kids begin to understand that other people can have different ideas or beliefs than themselves.

6 years old

The **gray matter** that makes up the outer layer of your brain has mostly finished growing by this age. Gray matter is made up of neurons. But the **axons** that form the connections between neurons will continue to grow and form through adolescence. Turn the page to find out more.

11 years old

Right around the end of this part of childhood (just before adolescence, which we'll get to on the next page), an area of your brain called the **prefrontal cortex** goes into a growth spurt. This is the part of your brain that helps with organization, memory, and planning.

Changes in Adolescence

Somewhere between ages 11 and 13, something amazing starts happening to your brain—and, let's face it—the rest of your body. You hit adolescence. If you're a boy your voice will start changing. You might notice your skin begin to breakout in acne. All of these events are controlled from your brain, which is undergoing some of the most incredible changes of all.

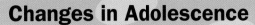

Growing and Pruning

During adolescence, the brain undergoes another big growth spurt, of nerve cells called neurons and the connections between them. What's interesting is that in addition to all of these new connections forming in your brain, there's a period of "pruning," in which your gray matter gets thinner. That's not a bad thing. It just means that the cells that are not being used don't get the nutrients they need, so they die off. This "use it or lose it" portion of adolescence creates a brain that works more efficiently. Some research has shown that during adolescence, there can be a loss of 1% of the gray matter until you reach your early 20s.

Dopamine Increase

When you hit adolescence, the neurons that produce a **chemical** called dopamine kick into high gear. Dopamine makes you focus on and respond to rewards. Some studies have shown that dopamine gets released in a teenager's brain when there's an exciting experience such as attending a cool concert, buying an amazing new pair of shoes, or playing a thrilling game. This can influence risk-taking behavior (we'll get to that in Chapter 4).

Myelination

In addition to the gray matter in your brain, you have **white matter**. White matter is made up of the axons that connect neurons to one another. During adolescence, your brain's white-matter connections get coated with a fatty material that **insulates** the connections. These coverings are called **myelin sheaths**. They let signals pass between the brain cells more efficiently, and with better coordination—kind of like upgrading from regular cable Internet to a super fiber optic cable, making the brain work more quickly.

myelin sheaths

THINK ABOUT IT!

What are some of the most important changes that happen in your brain during adolescence? Use your own words to explain these changes to a partner.

Brain Upgrade

Amygdala Under Construction

Your amygdala is a set of two small, almond-shaped neurons located on the front left and right sides of your brain. The amygdala helps connect your emotions to your memories. It is not fully myelinated, or insulated, until around your early 20s, When you're a teenager, it isn't completely connected to your frontal lobe. This may make it trickier for you to manage your emotions. The immature amygdala may also have an impact on decision-making, which we'll talk about in Chapter 4.

CHAPTER 2

Brain Changes in Your ENVIRONMENT

Throughout your life, your brain is in a constant state of motion. It's changing, developing, and adapting to the various information it receives throughout your day. In this chapter, you'll learn about how your brain is affected by both physical changes in the environment (the seasons), and also how our emotional relationships with others affect the ways our brains grow and develop.

Changing Seasons and the Brain

We all know that wonderful feeling we have when the sun is shining, the heat is on our skin, and we are spending lots of time outside. Experts believe that one of the biggest reasons we feel so happy in the summer months has to do with how our brain reacts to sunlight.

THINK ABOUT IT!

In the winter, do you feel sleepier? Do you sometimes feel sadder? Do you find that your mood changes? These are all symptoms that can be linked to the change in sunlight and can trigger different brain functioning.

There are two specific brain chemicals that are involved in feelings of sadness in the winter: **serotonin** and **melatonin**. These chemicals control our **sleep-wake cycles** and mood. Some researchers believe that decreased sunlight leads our brains to produce more melatonin, which makes us feel sleepier, and reduces our serotonin production, which is the key factor in helping us manage our emotions.

So what can you do to improve your brain function during the winter?

1. Spend more time outside! Take up some winter sports, such as snowshoeing, skiing, hiking, or simply taking a walk. This will not only boost the circulation of **endorphins** in your brain, making you feel happier, but you will be increasing your exposure to light, a key component in the creation of melatonin and serotonin in your brain.

2. Phototherapy. You can now buy special lamps to place on a tabletop or desk. You sit in front of it for about 45 minutes at a time with your eyes open. Your eyes need to be open as your retinas transmit the light's effects to your brain. Doing this every day for a few weeks will also help to relieve those "winter blues."

FAMILY MATTERS

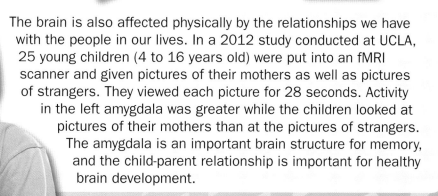

The brain is also affected physically by the relationships we have with the people in our lives. In a 2012 study conducted at UCLA, 25 young children (4 to 16 years old) were put into an fMRI scanner and given pictures of their mothers as well as pictures of strangers. They viewed each picture for 28 seconds. Activity in the left amygdala was greater while the children looked at pictures of their mothers than at the pictures of strangers. The amygdala is an important brain structure for memory, and the child-parent relationship is important for healthy brain development.

The Social World

Your prefrontal cortex is going through many major changes in adolescence, which may mean that you find yourself increasingly thinking about your mood and your emotions. Do you find yourself looking back and reflecting more on how you have reacted in certain social contexts, or situations? Are your reactions more impulsive or emotional than they were before? These experiences can feel scary or weird for teens. The important thing to know is that these changes are developmentally normal. The following sections will explain how your brain is developing and how this affects your social relationships. But most importantly, they will provide you with some strategies to better manage your relationships as you move through adolescence.

One area of brain research has looked into how teenagers are able to recognize different facial expressions, and the emotions on our faces. Some fMRI studies have shown heightened activity of the amygdala of teenagers (12–17-year-olds) versus adults, when responding to images of fearful faces. This may be why you notice yourself reacting more quickly and impulsively in social situations. Your amygdala is more sensitive to engaging in its fight-or-flight response, meaning that you don't get to use your prefrontal cortex to manage your emotions and impulse control. If you are more sensitive to seeing danger, for example, you are more likely to react with a defensive response.

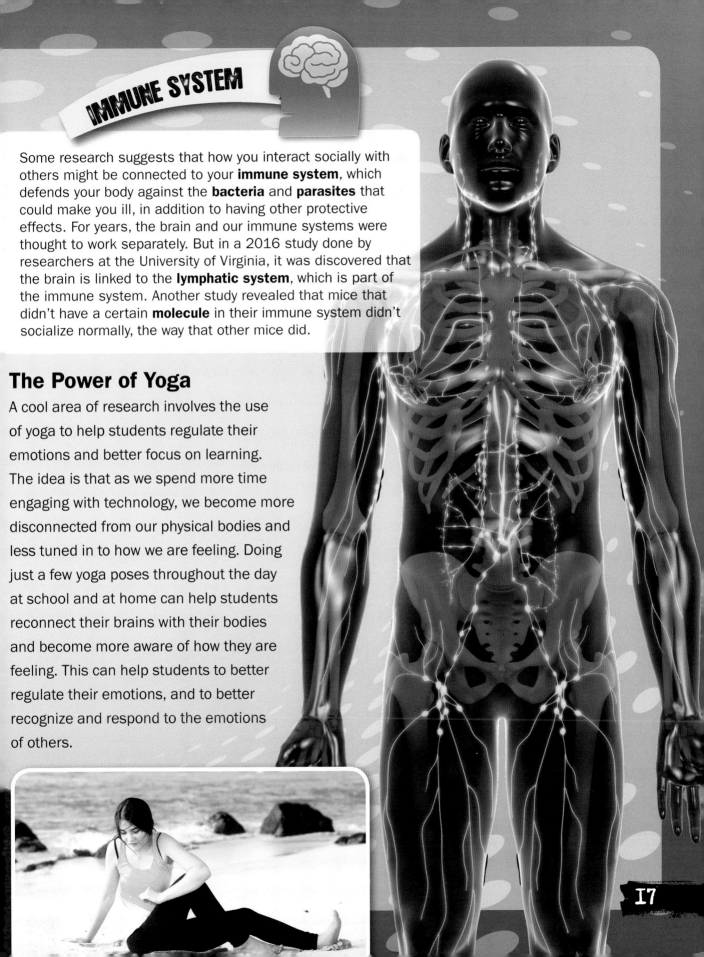

IMMUNE SYSTEM

Some research suggests that how you interact socially with others might be connected to your **immune system**, which defends your body against the **bacteria** and **parasites** that could make you ill, in addition to having other protective effects. For years, the brain and our immune systems were thought to work separately. But in a 2016 study done by researchers at the University of Virginia, it was discovered that the brain is linked to the **lymphatic system**, which is part of the immune system. Another study revealed that mice that didn't have a certain **molecule** in their immune system didn't socialize normally, the way that other mice did.

The Power of Yoga

A cool area of research involves the use of yoga to help students regulate their emotions and better focus on learning. The idea is that as we spend more time engaging with technology, we become more disconnected from our physical bodies and less tuned in to how we are feeling. Doing just a few yoga poses throughout the day at school and at home can help students reconnect their brains with their bodies and become more aware of how they are feeling. This can help students to better regulate their emotions, and to better recognize and respond to the emotions of others.

Your Brain Online

Chances are you spend a good amount of time not with your nose in a book like this, but on your phone using social media, or slaying your way through levels of a video game. Technology is ever-changing and makes our lives easier in many ways. But what are the effects of social media and video games on your developing brain?

Game On?

It's been estimated that if you're an avid gamer, by the time you turn 21 you'll have spent 10,000 hours mastering your skill. A lot has been written about how video games activate **visual-spatial skills**. These skills help you make sense of objects and pay attention to detail. However, a 2015 study at McGill University found that video-game players who spent at least six hours per week gaming were more likely to use **navigation** strategies motivated by the brain's reward system instead of the system used for spatial memory. This means that players are not using the part of the brain that remembers how the game looks—they are motivated by rewards instead. People who rely on this part of the brain don't have as much gray matter in the hippocampus, the part of the brain responsible for storing memories, as do those who use spatial memory.

hippocampus

THINK ABOUT IT!

What types of digital stimuli are you exposed to every day? Using the information you have learned about the relationship between your brain and its environment, what are some ways you think digital stimuli affects how you think or behave?

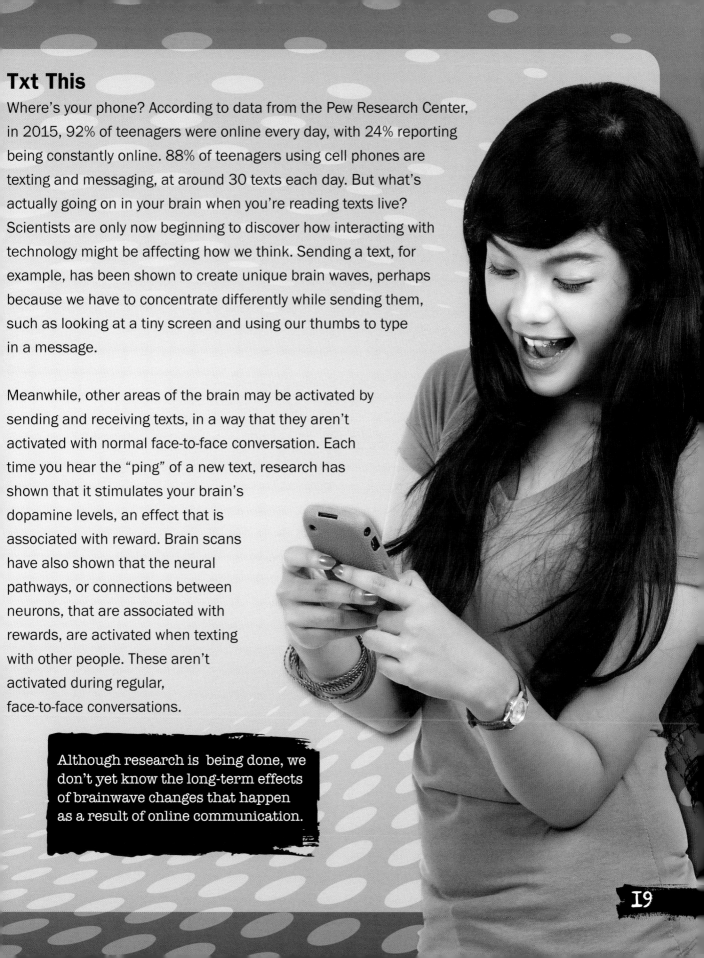

Txt This

Where's your phone? According to data from the Pew Research Center, in 2015, 92% of teenagers were online every day, with 24% reporting being constantly online. 88% of teenagers using cell phones are texting and messaging, at around 30 texts each day. But what's actually going on in your brain when you're reading texts live? Scientists are only now beginning to discover how interacting with technology might be affecting how we think. Sending a text, for example, has been shown to create unique brain waves, perhaps because we have to concentrate differently while sending them, such as looking at a tiny screen and using our thumbs to type in a message.

Meanwhile, other areas of the brain may be activated by sending and receiving texts, in a way that they aren't activated with normal face-to-face conversation. Each time you hear the "ping" of a new text, research has shown that it stimulates your brain's dopamine levels, an effect that is associated with reward. Brain scans have also shown that the neural pathways, or connections between neurons, that are associated with rewards, are activated when texting with other people. These aren't activated during regular, face-to-face conversations.

Although research is being done, we don't yet know the long-term effects of brainwave changes that happen as a result of online communication.

19

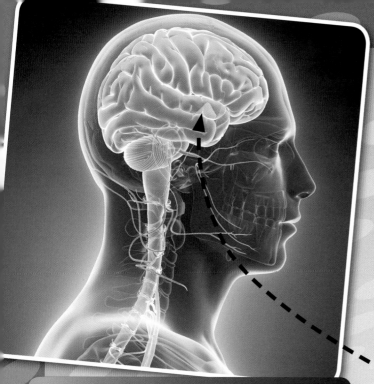

Managing Stress

When you are stressed, your hypothalamus signals your body to create hormones, which include **adrenaline**. This gets your heart hammering in your chest and the rest of your body goes into fight-or-flight mode. A little bit of stress certainly has the advantage of keeping you aware of danger. But dally stress can wear you down. What is the impact of this kind of stress on the body, and how does it affect your changing brain?

hypothalamus

BRAIN LAB

Take Five

One of the best ways to manage your emotions and help your brain to develop healthily is through mindful breathing exercises. This encourages your brain to access your prefrontal cortex, helping you to better manage your emotions and day-to-day living. So go on, take five!

Raise one of your hands and spread your fingers. Trace the outline of your hand with your index finger of the other hand, silently concentrating on the task. Keep tracing, but now take a breath in every time your index finger moves in the upward direction, and breathe out every time it moves downward. This helps guide your breathing and allows you to concentrate on the task of simply monitoring your breathing. Repeat this exercise a few times before engaging in a new task or when you start to feel anxious. You'll notice the effects pretty quickly afterward.

High Anxiety

Different parts of the brain develop and mature at different rates. The amygdala is the part of your brain that connects emotions to memories. It develops before your prefrontal cortex, which is the part of the brain associated with decision-making, being able to control impulses and social interactions, and **executive functioning**. This is the ability to know the difference between conflicting ideas, future goals, and long-term outcomes. You might already be able to understand how your present emotions can take over your long-term thoughts and goals, causing stress. For example, if you feel unprepared for an upcoming test, your amygdala might set your anxiety at a high level because of that one test—and you could lose sight of your larger goal, which is to pass your course with a B+.

Don't Fear the Square!

How in flux, or subject to change, is an adolescent's amygdala? There have been several interesting studies of this. In one study done in 2012, colored squares on a computer screen were shown to a group of participants that included kids, adolescents, and adults. One of the squares was shown at the same time as an annoying noise. People of all ages became used to seeing and hearing the square and the noise together. They showed a fear response in their brains when seeing the square, because their amygdalas connected seeing the square with the feeling of hearing the annoying sound.

Later, the researchers tried to get the participants to break the connection between the sound and the square by showing the square without the noise. Adolescents had a much harder time "unlearning" the connection between the noise and the square than did either the kids or the adults. This could be because the adolescents' amygdalas are further developed than other parts of the brain that deal with executive functioning.

EMOTIONAL Literacy and You

Although the amygdala develops before the prefrontal cortex, it is still not fully developed until a person is in their 20s. So, adolescents often face challenges managing, or controlling, their emotions. Can you control your emotions? Do you know and understand your own emotions, and can you identify and understand the emotions of others around you?

The questions fall under the umbrella of what is called emotional literacy. This term gets divided into two parts. The first part revolves around your ability to recognize your own emotions, to know how your body is feeling in relation to them, and how to react when feeling these emotions. The second part is external, and is a tricky part, recognizing those ranges of emotions in those around us, and changing our own behavior to help support others. Studies have shown that kids who can identify, understand, and respond to emotions in themselves and others engage in healthier friendships, more easily self-regulate, and learn to read at an earlier and more proficient level.

Emotional literacy involves three main skills:

Self-Awareness
awareness of your own emotions and behavior

Self-Management
the ability to handle your negative emotions

Relationship Management
the ability to work with others and foster positive relationships

Boosting Your Emotional Literacy

So what is the link between the brain and emotional literacy, and what kinds of things can you do to boost your own emotional literacy? Neuroplasticity is what we call the brain's ability to change, grow, and shape itself through exposure to a variety of experiences. The more the brain is exposed to certain experiences, the more connections it makes. Childhood and adolescence are the best times for neuroplasticity. Although this continues to happen throughout our lives, our neural networks grow or shrink most until we reach our mid-20s. That's why it's so important to start building your emotional literacy skills early.

Reading books that present new points of view and the emotions of their main characters, interacting with peers on group activities, and intramural sports, all help to shape the emotional and social network circuitry in our brains. To change these circuits and build positive habits, you need to be aware of and reflect on your own emotions and behaviors. Give the Brain Lab below a try. The activities are designed specifically to boost your emotional literacy.

BRAIN LAB

Strategies That Build Emotional Literacy

1. Keep a Feelings Journal: Do you keep a diary? Do you like doodling or writing? Consider keeping a feelings journal. This could take on various forms, either written in a notebook, drawn and illustrated, or verbally recorded on a phone or recording device. The medium doesn't matter. What is important is the self-reflection about how you felt in various situations. This will help you better understand how you reacted and how you coped, but also to recognize the range of feelings you had even in one experience. The more you self-reflect and explore the range of emotions you have over the day, the better you will be in approaching new social situations and challenges. Self-reflection like this actually stimulates the prefrontal cortex and enables you to store this knowledge in your long-term memory, building neural connections and improving your ability to deal with the world around you.

2. Feelings Collage: Don't like to write or say things out loud? A feelings collage or painting has the same effect. Think about a specific emotion or experience you would like to show artistically, either through cutting and pasting or drawing images that resonate with you, to create a work of art that reflects the range of emotions you have felt. So go on, get creative!

You might be wondering why emotional literacy is so important. Since your amygdala isn't fully developed, building your emotional literacy can be a challenge. But there's good news! Your emotional literacy can be improved with practice. Here are a few tips and strategies that may help you in your day-to-day life.

Emotional Awareness

One way to work on your emotional intelligence is simply to catalog and be aware of your emotions, and how you're feeling, as you're going through your day. You can get so caught up in what is happening during the day (Math test! Hungry for lunch! Work on literacy activity! Text BFF about after-school plans!) that you may not notice your own emotions. As a strategy, try to think about how you are feeling, even putting labels on your feelings throughout the day (e.g., "I feel frustrated when Mom gives me a tuna sandwich for lunch... maybe I should make my own lunch from now on...").

THINK ABOUT IT!

Can you think of another strategy that would help you develop emotional literacy in your day-to-day life? Share your strategy with a friend.

24

Try to Limit Your Negative Emotions

Throughout your day, you will have negative thoughts. Maybe you're thinking about how much you hate the soggy cereal you ate for breakfast, or worrying about why you didn't get a text back from a friend—are they ignoring me? But changing the way you think about a situation can actually change the way you feel about it. Is that friend actually ignoring you, or is he or she just busy? This also helps you improve how you interact with others. Instead of being upset with that friend because you felt ignored, you might see the situation from their perspective and ask them about their busy day.

Don't React... Respond

When someone does something you don't like, such as interrupting you in a conversation, what do you do? Snap back at him or her in annoyance? Reacting like that is when you've been triggered emotionally, and relieve that emotion by getting it out of your system in a quick, easy way.

But it's not the same as responding. Responding involves first actually thinking about, and being aware of, how you're feeling. Then, you decide how you will communicate. Can you express your frustration in a way that doesn't involve raising your voice or speaking rudely to the other person? Can you listen to the other person's point of view, and respond in a way that values what the other person said?

You DECIDE...

Earlier, you read about some of the physical changes taking place in your brain, such as pruning, myelination, and an increase in dopamine. Each of these is a normal development in the brain—but they can pose some challenges when it comes to your decision-making. You make decisions every day on what you will do and how you will think. Knowing all of these physical changes that you're going through and understanding the challenges they pose can help you take control and make decisions that will help you in the future.

The Prefrontal Cortex and Executive Control

Although your brain was nearly adult-sized during childhood, there is still one part that needs to mature: the prefrontal cortex, located in the frontal lobe in the spot behind your forehead. During adolescence, your prefrontal cortex continues to change—and won't finish maturing until you're well into your 20s. This part of your brain controls your executive functioning, decision-making, and how you take control of your emotions and self-regulate. For example, having the knowledge about what's right and wrong, and making a decision about it, are two separate processes. Your executive functioning involves the latter process.

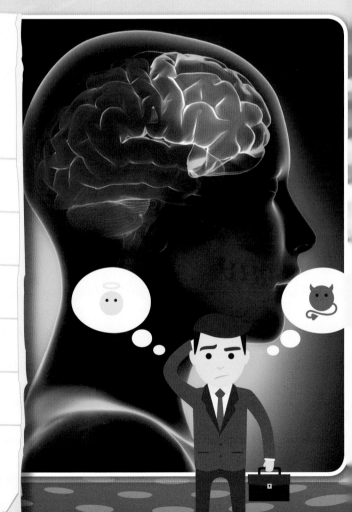

Get Limbic

To understand a bit more about how your decision-making thinking works, we'll need to explore your **limbic system**. This is a set of structures that work together within the brain. They include the hippocampus, the frontal cortex, the hypothalamus, and the amygdala (for more information, see page 42). These parts of your brain are responsible for your long-term memories, as well as for your behavior and emotions—things that start to change and shift as you move through adolescence. Do you like taking crazy risks? Like doing an awesome flip on your skateboard, or some Ninja Warrior-style acrobatics? That rush you get from risky behavior is from your limbic system in action. In adolescents, the limbic system is much more sensitive than it is in adults.

Out of Balance

Since your decision-making is regulated by your reward system as well as by your prefrontal cortex, there are two systems at play when you're making decisions. Adults, with their mature prefrontal cortex, tend to avoid risky behavior that adolescents may indulge in. But your still-developing prefrontal cortex isn't telling you to stop doing something silly. Adults may show a greater balance between these two systems: being rewarded, and knowing when a decision is too risky (e.g., don't slide down that railing—it may be fun, but it's dangerous!).

One theory is that your reward system and your prefrontal cortex are not maturing at the same rate, causing an imbalance. This imbalance theory is the disconnect or mismatch between having a more maturing reward system but less mature frontal lobe. In younger children both systems are at an immature stage, and adults have them at a mature stage. Teenagers getting involved in risky behavior (drinking alcohol, driving without a seatbelt, fights after school) have a super-sensitive reward system (limbic system) along with an underdeveloped prefrontal cortex.

Your underdeveloped prefrontal cortex might not immediately tell you that performing tricks on your bike—without a helmet—isn't a good idea.

Face-Off

What happens when adolescent impulsivity is put to the test? There have been some interesting studies of this. In one, 83 people aged 6 to 29 were shown a group of faces on a computer monitor. The faces were either neutral or scary. Participants were told to hit a button if they saw a neutral face. They were told to not hit the button if the face was scary. When scary faces appeared, adolescents made more mistakes by hitting the button than both the adults and the kids in the study.

BRAIN LAB

Decision-Making Game

Follow these steps to play a decision-making game with some friends. The more practice you have talking and thinking about complex decisions and situations, the better you will be able to make them in real-life situations.

1. Sit in two circles, one within the other. You should be facing one another.
2. The inner circle moves counter-clockwise, while the outer circle moves clockwise.
3. Make someone the leader who calls "stop" to decide which new partner you face.
4. The leader asks the question that everyone has to discuss with their partner face-to-face.
5. Go from easy questions such as "What's the best ice cream?" to hard questions that involve more debatable ideas.
6. Keep rotating and asking new questions for discussion.

Here are some great questions to use:
1. Your friend has asked you to keep a secret that you feel is unsafe. Do you tell someone and break your friend's trust, or keep the secret?
2. Your friend has made you very upset and angry, but you know that they are going through some rough times at home with their family. Do you share how you are feeling?

Long-Term Planning and Goal-Directed Behaviors

You've read a lot now about how your changing prefrontal cortex and limbic system affect your emotional regulation and decision-making, but these brain changes also affect your ability to plan out long-term tasks and goals. Since the adolescent brain is more likely to respond to instant rewards or worries, it can be difficult to see past immediate stimuli and plan for long-term goals. All of these skills are rapidly changing and developing during adolescence. They need to be practiced regularly to make the neural connections that you will use throughout your adult life.

The challenges to your decision-making skills might sound concerning—and they can be, in some situations. But the good news is that you can take action by using strategies that help support the skills and behaviors that are still being developed.

What's Your End Goal?

Long-term goal-setting is essential in all areas of your life. It can help keep your mind off the instant rewards influenced by the high levels of dopamine in your brain. Try sketching out a long-term goal. For example, you might want to increase your average at school by 5% or be made captain of your soccer team. Then, break your goal down into the smaller actions needed to reach it. These smaller goals can help direct your thoughts and actions.

Start here ⟶

Write your long-term goal here

Write what you have to do to achieve the goal you wrote above.

Write what you have to do to reach the goal you wrote above.

Write what you have to do to get to the goal you wrote above.

Write what you have to do to get to the goal you wrote above.

To-Do List

1. Homework
8. Put away laundry
7. Clean room
4. Help Dad with backyard
6. Take out the trash
2. Class Project
5. Return book to library
9. Call Jen back about movie
3. Soccer practice

Prioritize!

Huge to-do lists often overwhelm people. This is especially true for adolescents like you, whose prefrontal cortex—the part of the brain that controls planning—is still developing. Try using this method to prioritize your work. To prioritize means to choose to complete certain things before others.

Brainstorm all of the activities you need to complete this week, such as homework, sports, events, volunteer work, or social commitments. Write them down on a piece of paper. Then, rank the activities from most important to least important—with one being the most important. Then, you can tackle your to-do list in that order.

Communication Filter

Even though it might not feel like it, you are in complete control of how you respond to situations around you. Training yourself to stop and filter your communications can help limit misunderstandings, hurt feelings, or other conflict.

RESPECT
How would I feel if these words were spoken to me?

EMPATHY
Can I see what happened through another person's point of view?

CHOICE
Is this something that needs to be said?

LISTEN
Did I give the other person a chance to explain or apologize?

CHAPTER 4

BRAIN CARE

Now that you know a bit more about how your brain is in the process of changing, how are you going to take care of it? One of the easiest ways to ensure that your control hub is working well is to take care of your body with regular exercise. Working out isn't just for muscles! Exercise has benefits that give you a big brain boost.

Walking and Creative Thinking

Step by step, that's all it can take to improve your cognitive and creative **capacities**...literally! Research studies have shown that creative thinking improves while a person is walking and shortly thereafter, according to a study co-authored by Marily Oppezzo, and Daniel Schwartz at Stanford University. The study found that walking indoors or outdoors similarly boosted creative inspiration. The act of walking itself, and not the environment, was the main factor. Across the board, creativity levels were consistently and significantly higher for those walking compared to those sitting. So put on your walking shoes and get moving!

The Daily Mile
In the United Kingdom, schools are signing up to be part of a new movement called the Daily Mile. The goal is to have all students at each school running or walking for at least 15 minutes before the start of class every day. The effects have been proven to improve academic and social success. So go on, why not see whether you can convince your own school to take on the Daily Mile challenge.

Go Ahead, Be Bored

Yes, that's right. Maybe you're so overprogrammed with school and after-school activities that you actually need some time to sit around and just be bored. And we're not talking sit-at-your-computer bored, but really bored, with screens off (because, according to 2016 Nielsen research, Americans spend around 10 hours a day consuming media of some kind). There's even some research to support this finding. In a 2014 study in the UK, 80 subjects were given boring tasks, such as reading and copying down stuff from the phone book. When they were asked to come up with creative ways to use plastic cups, they tended to come up with more creative ways than those who weren't given a boring task.

Need for Sleep

In a perfect world, you should spend about one-third of your life sleeping. Although there's no answer for why we sleep, researchers believe that sleep helps to strengthen neural connections formed during the day, as well as get rid of the unimportant ones, and helps the brain to get rid of any waste products. Some research suggests that sleep is the time that your brain uses to store memories. But in our highly **stimulated** world, with all of its distractions, are you getting enough sleep? How much is enough? And what happens when you don't?

How Much?

How much sleep do you need to get through your day? According to the National Sleep Foundation, school-aged children (6–13 years) should be getting anywhere between 9 and 11 hours per night, while teenagers (14–17 years) need slightly less at 8 to 10 hours, to feel fully rested. As you age, you'll need slightly less sleep, but anything less than 6 hours can cause problems.

So, what happens when you're not sleeping enough? What effect does this have on the brain? Scientists are still trying to figure out the long-term impacts of sleep deprivation. Less sleep means less activity in the frontal and parietal lobes of the brain, which are important for memory and problem-solving.

Brain Shrink

Not getting enough sleep isn't just going to leave you feeling foggy—it could also shrink your brain over time. Studies using rats have shown that disrupted sleep makes the brain's hippocampus grow smaller. A lack of sleep also affected neurogenesis, which is the process by which more neurons are made in the brain. A 2010 study found that sleep disruption in humans was linked with reduced volume in the hippocampus.

NEWBORNS (0–2 MONTHS)
12 to 18 HOURS

INFANTS (3–11 MONTHS)
14 to 15 HOURS

TODDLER (1–3 YEARS)
12 to 14 HOURS

PRESCHOOLERS (3–5 YEARS)
11 to 13 HOURS

SCHOOL AGE (5–10)
10 to 11 HOURS

TEENS (11–17 YEARS)
8.5 to 9.5 HOURS

BRAIN LAB

Sleep Hygiene

Is it challenging for you to get to sleep some nights? There are many reasons why you might toss and turn at bedtime. Did you know that you can actually prepare your body to sleep by winding down your body and mind? Try these preparation strategies and monitor how they work for you.

- Stop technology use at least one hour before bedtime.
- Avoid drinking caffeine, such as coffee or soda.
- Exercise during the day—but not too close to bedtime!
- Create a bedtime routine. Doing the same routine before going to bed can help your body recognize that it's time to sleep. Activities might include reading, taking a hot shower, or some light stretching.

You Are What You Eat

The foods you eat can certainly help give you a brain booster, particularly in the morning when you're gearing up for a busy day at school or work.

Fish and Nuts

Full of omega-3 fatty acids such as DHA, which helps to lubricate the brain or make it run smoothly. These acids may also help combat diseases such as dementia and Alzheimer's later in life. Our neurons need these fats to work properly.

Chicken

The leaner, the better. The protein in chicken gives you the **amino acids** you need to produce neurotransmitters.

Fruits and Vegetables

Dark, leafy veggies are great. Spinach, for instance, is not only high in protein, but has proven to be a good brain booster. In one study done at the University of South Florida, rats that were fed a spinach-heavy diet learned faster than ones that didn't eat spinach. Also good for you are blueberries. In addition to vitamins, they're loaded with **antioxidants** and acetylcholine—a chemical used in your brain for learning and memory.

Pasta, Cereal, Bread

The **complex carbohydrates** in these foods can give you a big energy boost. According to a study done at MIT University, carbohydrates from these foods may also help you produce a chemical called serotonin, which can keep you in a good mood.

Better Eat Breakfast

Thinking about a sugary breakfast, or skipping it altogether? You may want to think again. That was the subject of a 2003 study in the U.K., in which 30 kids and youths aged 9 to 16 either had soft drinks for breakfast (sugary simple carbohydrates), a traditional breakfast with complex carbohydrates (e.g., toast, cereal), or no breakfast. A few hours later, researchers tested the kids' abilities to recall a series of numbers to see how they did with memory skills. The kids who had the sugary drinks had a poorer reaction time than those who ate cereal. In fact, they were responding with the reaction times of 70-year-olds!

A different study found that breakfasting on some proteins may make for an even better choice. Young people who had beans versus toast did better on memory tests as the questions became more and more difficult.

Taking Care of Your Mental Health

Being a teen can be a very busy, stressful, and emotionally demanding time in your life. Many parts of your body are undergoing changes, and you are being given greater freedoms—but with increasing responsibilities. Also, new research indicates that teens' increasing use of technology and social media means that you are constantly experiencing social stress, making it more difficult to focus on yourself and your own well-being. That's why it's so important to learn about your own mental health and how you can put great supports and strategies in place to help you feel physically and emotionally well.

According to the United States Department of Health & Human Services and the Canadian Mental Health Association, the term "mental health" refers to our emotional, psychological, and social well being. The well-being of our minds affects how we think, feel, and act—and also how we respond to stress, relate to others, and make choices. We all have mental health, and it is extremely important to take care of it.

Research shows that one in every four to five young people in the United States, and 10 to 20 % of young Canadians, are affected by a serious mental illness—one that hurts their ability to function as they usually would. Even more youth are affected by other disorders, such as anxiety. This means that you or your friends may experience some level of mental-health difficulty throughout adolescence. The key is to learn what mental health is and how you can support yourself through great habits, but also how to access support when you need it.

If you have any questions or concerns, make sure to talk to someone, whether a family member, a health care professional, a teacher, or a friend. The first step in addressing your mental health is sharing with someone how you are feeling. Often, these experiences can leave you feeling as though you are the only one struggling, but this is not the case. The earlier you talk about it, the easier it is to get help.

Positive Self-Talk

How you think about things has a powerful effect on your well-being. Self-talk describes the thoughts we have about ourselves and the situations we face. Positive self-talk can make you see things in a more hopeful way. It can make you more likely to try to change or improve things. Positive self-talk is a good way to help you take care of your mental health on a daily basis. Try these strategies to work on your positive self-talk.

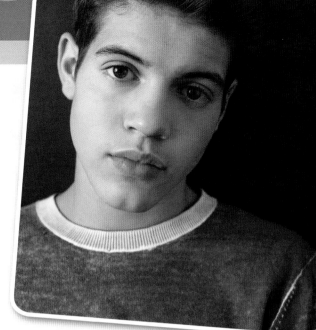

1. Find a quiet place and pay attention to your self-talk. Are your thoughts positive, or are they discouraging?

2. Try to notice when you are using negative self-talk. Think of ways you can change your thoughts to make them more positive. For example, you could avoid using the words "never" or "everyone" when you face a problem. These words can make the problem seem bigger than it really is. Write down ways that work for you.

3. Be a friend to yourself. Think about how you might respond to a friend who is experiencing a challenge. Talk to yourself in the same positive way.

Daily Mind Dump

A good way to take care of your mental health is to say or write down your feelings each day. Getting your feelings out there can help you make sense of your emotions or see things in a new way.

Use this strategy to get your feelings off your chest each day. It can be done in a journal, recorded on a phone or recording device, or spoken to someone whose job is strictly to listen. Take five minutes at the end of your day to jot down or say out loud everything that bothered you or that is floating around in your mind.

Into Adulthood...

As you've learned, your brain will still be maturing until about your mid-20s. At about age 30, your brain is at its peak cognitive powers, with a fully formed prefrontal cortex. Now you can start to make the kinds of adult decisions that involve balancing your emotions with your understanding of the effects your decisions can have. But what happens to the brain as you continue to age, especially now that people are living longer and longer lives?

The Aging Brain

As you age, your brain ages, too. And that means that it will begin to lose the neurons that can't be replaced. By the time you hit about 55 years of age, parts of the brain (such as the prefrontal cortex and the hippocampus) begin to get smaller—by about 1% to 2% each year. This means that an aging brain sees some cognitive decline, such as in long-term and working memory. It might take an older person longer to store and retrieve information, or to concentrate on what he or she is thinking about.

Young Vs Old

Some research has examined how the brains of older and younger people take in information. When looking at pictures, younger people tend to activate the visual cortex. As you get older, brain scans have shown that both hemispheres of the brain are activated at about the same level.

THINK ABOUT IT!

Using information you have learned in this book, make a list of some of the ways that you can keep your brain healthy as you continue to grow. Which of these ways do you already use? Which could you start using?

The Good News

As new research is showing, the brain continues to be able to form new connections between existing neurons. So, while focus and shifts in attention might be more challenging for an aging brain, the ability to remember information can be retained. Think about it this way—a young person might remember most of the little that they know, but an older person knows more, and may only forget some of it. Some research has pointed to the benefits of distractions on an aging brain in people over age 50. This might help with solving problems and learning new information, because numerous types of tasks (that shifts in attention demand) require a broad attention span, instead of a more focused one.

3 Ways to Keep an Aging Brain in Shape

1. **Learn a New Language**
   Some studies have shown that regardless of age, learning a new language can help increase connections in the brain.

2. **Keep Exercising**
   Some studies have supported the idea that exercise (e.g., walking on a treadmill) could improve executive functioning in the elderly. A 2016 study suggested that a regular exercise routine could slow the effects of aging on the brain by 10 years.

3. **Enjoy Arts and Crafts**
   A four-year study (published in 2015) involved more than 250 people over the age of 87. Those participants who were actively involved in arts and crafts activities (e.g., painting, drawing, quilting) were 73% less likely to show mild cognitive impairments than those who did not participate in arts or crafts.

WRAP IT UP!

Your brain changes throughout your life. It grows new connections and gets rid of others. It can even physically rearrange as you learn new skills! Adolescence is one of the most important—and challenging—times in brain development. But the good news is that you can arm yourself with strategies that promote positive personal and brain development during your adolescent years. The diagram on this page shows some of the parts of the brain at play when we talk about what's going on in an adolescent's brain.

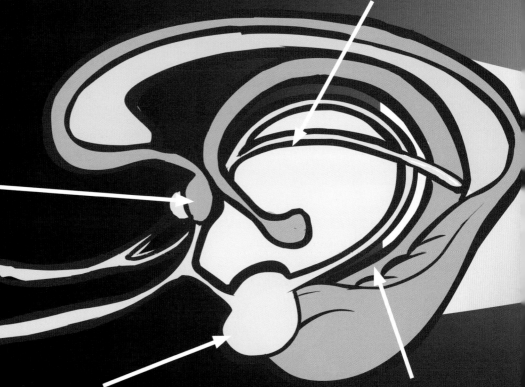

Thalamus – This relays messages from your senses to the **cerebrum**, where your brain can respond to the messages it receives.

Hypothalamus – This part of the brain controls how **glands** give off hormones that help you grow, digest food, and perform other functions. It regulates some autonomic activities in your brain, which are those that you do not actively control.

Amygdala – This part of the brain controls your emotional reactions to stimuli and events.

Hippocampus – The hippocampus stores long-term and short-term memories. It also works to connect your memories with emotions, based on your past experiences.

PREFRONTAL CORTEX

This all-important part of your brain allows you to make decisions, think critically, and learn complex new things. It is also the part of your brain in control of your executive-functioning skills. It doesn't finish developing until your 20s.

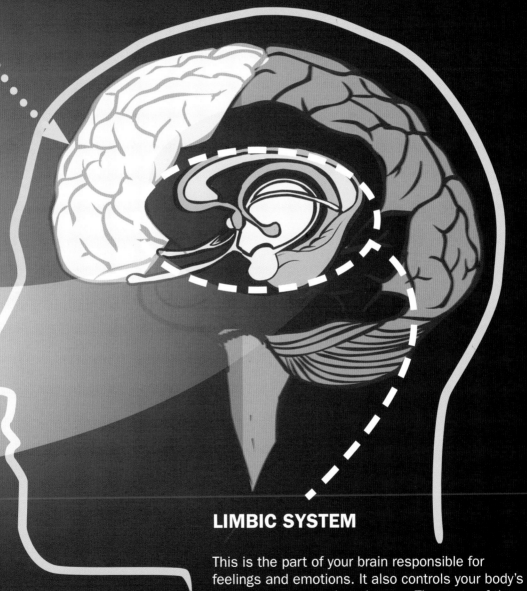

LIMBIC SYSTEM

This is the part of your brain responsible for feelings and emotions. It also controls your body's drives or urges, such as hunger. The parts of the limbic system play such an important role in how your brain works during adolescence that we've broken some of them down on the left.

43

BIBLIOGRAPHY

BOOKS

Costandi, Moheb. *Neuroplasticity*. The MIT Press, 2016.

Eisen, Michael and Jeffrey. *Empowered YOUth: A Father and Son's Journey to Conscious Living*. Hay House, 2012.

Klingberg, Torkel, MD, PhD. *The Learning Brain: Memory and Brain Development in Children*. Oxford University Press, 2013.

The Adolescent Brain: Learning, Reasoning, and Decision Making, edited by Valery F. Reyna, Sandra B. Chapman, Michael R. Dougherty and Jere Confrey, American Psychological Association, Washington D.C., 2012.

Sweeney, Michael S. *Brain: The Complete Mind*. National Geographic, 2009.

WEBSITES

fmri.ucsd.edu/Research/whatisfmri.html

www.mayfieldclinic.com/PE-EEG.htm

www.pbs.org/wgbh/pages/frontline/shows/teenbrain/work/adolescent.html

www.acpeds.org/the-college-speaks/position-statements/parenting-issues/the-teenage-brain-under-construction

www.theatlantic.com/health/archive/2014/01/dopamine-and-teenage-logic/282895/

www.macleans.ca/society/life/inside-your-teenagers-scary-brain/

www.bbc.co.uk/science/0/21685448

www.newscientist.com/article/mg20227022-900-the-five-ages-of-the-brain-adolescence/

www.mayoclinic.org/healthy-lifestyle/adult-health/expert-answers/how-many-hours-of-sleep-are-enough/faq-20057898

www.yogajournal.com/poses/yoga-for/kids

www.huffingtonpost.com/amy-brann/the-neuroscience-of-emotional-intelligence_b_9331292.html

www.danielgoleman.info/daniel-goleman-the-case-for-teaching-emotional-literacy-in-schools-2/

www.creativeyouthideas.com/resources/icebreakers/scruples-shuffle/#ixzz51QuPj9aa

https://cmha.ca/media/fast-facts-about-mental-illness/

www.mentalhealth.gov/basics/what-is-mental-health

https://childmind.org/topics/concerns/depression/

http://time.com/magazine/us/4547305/november-7th-2016-vol-188-no-19-u-s/

http://youthwellnessnetwork.ca/about_us/michael_eisen_ywn_founder/

ACADEMIC STUDIES (Selected)

Choudhury S, Blakemore S-J, Charman T. "Social cognitive development during adolescence." Social cognitive and affective neuroscience. 2006;1(3):165-174. doi:10.1093/scan/nsl024.

Erickson KI, Gildengers AG, Butters MA. "Physical activity and brain plasticity in late adulthood." Dialogues in Clinical Neuroscience. 2013;15(1):99-108.

Filiano AJ, Xu Y, Tustison NJ, et al. "Unexpected role of interferon-y in regulating neuronal connectivity and social behavior." Nature. 2016;535(7612):425-429. doi:10.1038/nature18626.

Mann, Sandi & Cadman, Rebekah. (2014). "Does Being Bored Make Us More Creative?." Creativity Research Journal. 26. 165-173. 10.1080/10400419.2014.901073.

Tatum, William O. et al. "Cortical processing during smartphone text messaging." Epilepsy & Behavior , Volume 59 , 117 - 121

Tottenham, N., Shapiro, M., Telzer, E., & Humphreys, K. (2012). "Amygdala response to mother." Developmental Science, 15(3), 307-19.

West GL, Drisdelle BL, Konishi K, Jackson J, Jolicoeur P, Bohbot VD. "Habitual action video game playing is associated with caudate nucleus-dependent navigational strategies." 2015. Proc. R. Soc. B 282:20142952.

LEARNING MORE

BOOKS

Deak, JoAnn and Terrence Deak. *The Owner's Manual for Driving Your Adolescent Brain*. Little Pickle Press, 2013.

Freedman, Jeri. *Your Beautiful Brain: Keeping Your Brain* Healthy. Rosen Publishing Company, 2013.

Spalding, Maddie. *12 Tips to Maintain Brain Health*. RiverStream Publishing, 2016.

WEBSITES

Read about the adolescent brain and the stories of teens who use mindfulness to make a difference.
www.mindful.org/amazing-tumultuous-wild-wonderful-teenage-brain/

Check out and try some of these "Mental Fitness Tips" from the Canadian Mental Health Association.
https://cmha.ca/resources/mental-fitness-tips/#.VV_ZtZRIUUM

This helpful website shares tips, tricks, and information to help you develop the skills you need to succeed, such as recognizing and managing emotions and stress.
www.skillsyouneed.com/ps/managing-emotions.html

GLOSSARY

adrenaline A hormone produced by the body during times of stress. Adrenaline increases breathing rates and blood circulation rates, and prepares the muscles in the body to flee.

amino acids The substances that make up proteins—nutrients that are essential for helping our cells function

antioxidants Substances that reduce or stop chemical reactions caused by oxygen

axons The long, threadlike part of a neuron that sends messages to other neurons

bacteria Tiny living organisms that can be harmful, such as when they cause illness or infection, or helpful, such as when they help digestion

brain imaging technologies The different methods used to produce images of the brain

capacities Our abilities to do something

cells Tiny units, or parts, that make up living things

cerebrum A large part of the brain that takes in messages from our senses, stores memories, and helps with emotions. It is made up of the outer layer of the brain and some parts of the inner brain.

chemical A new substance that is formed when two or more substances interact

complex carbohydrates Commonly found in whole plant foods, such as grains and vegetables, complex carbohydrates are made of many sugar molecules put together. They are much healthier for humans than simple carbohydrates, which are made of just one or two sugar molecules.

dendrites The short, branch-like fibers that extend from the body of a nerve cell, and which receive and transmit messages to the nerve cell from other nerve cells

electrodes Small pieces of metal or other substances through which electricity enters or leaves an object

electroencephalography A method of recording electrical activity in the brain

endorphins Hormones in the brain that lessen or stop pain, and increase pleasure

functional magnetic resonance imaging A method of recording blood flow in the brain

glands Organs or groups of cells that make substances that the body needs

gray matter Darker tissue of the brain that contains cell bodies of neurons and their dendrites

immune system The system that protects the body from outside substances that could cause illness

insulates Surrounds to protect

lymphatic system Part of the circulatory system, which transports nutrients and other substances around the body, the lymphatic system helps keep fluid at the right balance in the body

melatonin A hormone that helps regulate sleep-wake cycles

molecule Two or more atoms chemically bonded together

motor region Part of the cerebrum or cerebral cortex that controls our body movements

myelin sheaths The fatty substances that encase axons or nerve fibers. The extensions—axons and dendrites—of neurons, that connect them to each other.

navigation The process of directing a route or understanding one's place or position

neurons Nerve cells

oxygen The gas we breathe to live

parasites Living organisms that live off another living thing, and offer no benefit in return

positron emission tomography (PET) A method of brain imaging that generates images of tissues and organs. It involves a person swallowing a type of drug that helps the tissue or organ show up on the camera.

prefrontal cortex Part of the cerebrum that is involved with our executive functioning skills

radioactive Describes something that emits radiation, a type of energy

serotonin A chemical in the brain that affects how we feel and our sleep-wake cycle

stimulated Raised level of response or action

sleep-wake cycles The cyclical, or recurring, patterns of sleep and wakefulness

syringe A device used to inject substances into the body, or draw out substances such as blood

visual-spatial skills Skills that help us understand the relationships between objects we see

white matter The lighter brain tissue that connects the gray matter areas and carries signals between neurons

INDEX

About the Authors

Jeff Szpirglas and Danielle Saint-Onge work as authors and teachers. Jeff has written numerous books for young readers focusing on themes such as fear, and unusual human behavior. He is also passionate about horror stories. When taking a break from being the school librarian and writing books, Danielle runs her own private coaching practice. She works one-on-one with children and families experiencing executive functioning difficulties. Both Jeff and Danielle are passionate educators who believe in writing books that reflect the experiences and lives of the students they teach.